MUST TRY HARDER!

History

Constable & Robinson Ltd
55-56 Russell Square
London WC1B 4HP

www.constablerobinson.com

First published in the UK in 2013 by Constable,
an imprint of Constable & Robinson Ltd

Text © Constable & Robinson 2013
Compiled by Mark Leigh, Rod Green, Diane Law and Mike Haskins
Additional illustrations © 2013 Leah Barker

A copy of the British Library Cataloguing in Publication Data is
available from the British Library

ISBN 978-1-47211-380-1

Printed and bound by CPI Group (UK) Ltd, Croydon, CR0 4YY

10 9 8 7 6 5 4 3 2 1

MUST TRY HARDER!

History

A. N. Teacher

INTRODUCTION

Your schooldays, however fondly you may remember them, are a minefield of potential classroom gaffes for students who are particularly naïve or who don't keep their wits about them. If it's true that we learn by making mistakes, then there are some poor pupils who must surely have been approaching genius level by the time they finally left the school gates behind forever, and it would seem that this has been the case ever since teachers first started chalking questions on a blackboard. Exam and homework blunders have provided endless amusement over the years with many appearing in print, the 19th century "Bulls and Blunders" being one early example. Such anthologies were especially popular in the 1930s, with Cecil Hunt's *Howlers* and Alexander Abingdon's *Boners* collections (illustrated by Dr Seuss) selling around the world, and inspiring many imitations.

The origins of these collections were complex. Clearly school teachers have always encountered weird and wacky mistakes on a daily basis – but sometimes they also turned these into teaching tools (what better way to bang home the right answer than to start with an example of a catastrophic mistake!) or adapted them for humorous purposes.

Today, our teachers continue to collect and share the most bizarre answers they find. Part of the joy of reading these comes from wondering what really happened. Is this a pupil desperately grasping for a half-remembered fact, or a surreal example of startling ignorance? Or is the student giving a knowingly cheeky, absurd answer, which might or might not amuse the teacher?

Either way, these blunders provide an ongoing source of fun. Here is the latest set of dispatches from the chalkface, in this case from the dim and distant region of History, a place no-one can ever visit and whose mistakes we appear doomed to repeat . . .

HISTORY

What caused the Titanic to
sink in 1912?

Water

What was introduced during
the First World War to speed up
agricultural production?

Runner beans

MUST TRY HARDER

Why was Hadrian's wall built?

Because Hadrian's fence fell down.

In 1965 which army did the Americans fight against in North Vietnam?

The King Kong

HISTORY

Name one cause of the Wall
Street Crash.

Bad drivers

Where was the Magna Carta signed?

At the bottom

MUST TRY HARDER

What was the most famous discovery made during the Bronze Age?

Suntan lotion

What were the circumstances of Archbishop Cranmer's death?

Henry VIII had him burned on a steak.

Name the wife of Zeus, who was the goddess of women and marriage.

Mrs Zeus

What did Ferdinand Magellan's Spanish expedition achieve in 1522?

The first circumcision of the globe.

Name one gangster who flourished during Prohibition.

Bugsy Malone

When was William Shakespeare born?

on his birthday

HISTORY

In 1815 who did the Duke of Wellington defeat at the Battle of Waterloo?

Linoleum Bonaparte

How did sailors calculate their latitude in the Tudor period?

With their smartphones

MUST TRY HARDER

What was bootlegging?

A kind of shoe polish

What do Mahatma Gandhi and the Dalai Lama have in common?

Names that are hard to spell

What was Aphrodite the goddess of?

Big hair

What did Queen Victoria become on her 40th birthday?

40

How did Ludwig von Beethoven overcome his deafness when composing his 9th symphony?

He played louder

List one similarity between Alexander the Great and Richard the Lionheart.

They had the same middle name

What were the women who campaigned for the vote known as?

The suffer jets

Who succeeded the first President of the United States, George Washington?

The second President of the United States.

Which term is sometimes used to describe the USA in the 1920s?

Crazy!

How did Viking longboats communicate with each other when at sea?

Norse code

HISTORY

Describe what happened to the English crown following the death of Henry V?

It fell off his head

What is the meaning of free trade?

When they don't charge you for listing stuff on Ebay.

MUST TRY HARDER

Who was Prime Minister of Great Britain for most of the Second World War?

Adolf Hitler

Who won the Battle of Hastings?

Will. I. Am the Conker and his Viking hoard.

What was Magna Carta?

She was the first woman Prime minister

What were the main advantages of the open field method of farming?

It was easier for the farmer to get his tractor into the field

MUST TRY HARDER

What was the name given to the
rulers of ancient Egypt?

 The fairies

Describe one of the main causes of
the end of the Cold War.

Global warming

HISTORY

How was Guy Fawkes punished for trying to blow up the Houses of Parliament in the Gunpowder Plot?

They put him in a big milk bottle and fired him into the sky.

Explain why Florence Nightingale was known as the 'Lady with the Lamp'?

She had a lamp

What strategic errors contributed to the failure of the Charge of the Light Brigade?

They were too easy to see in the dark

What was celebrated for only the second time in British history by the present Queen in 2012?

Sex

HISTORY

How did Gandhi dress at the Round Table Conference? What was the significance of this?

He wore a lioncloth. So everyone knew he'd caught a lion.

Why was the U2 Crisis in 1960 a challenge to Khrushchev's policy of peaceful co-existence?

Because their music was so awful.

MUST TRY HARDER

From the 8th century Viking invaders began arriving in Britain in longships. Where did they come from?

A door in the side of the longship

Describe the difference between the February Revolution and the October Revolution.

8 months

Where was Henry VIII crowned?

On his head

Name one of the Ancient Greeks' greatest achievements.

Learning to speak Greek.

What was the result of the Battle
of Waterloo?

Abba won the Eurovision Song Contest

Whereabouts was King Harold
injured at the Battle of Hastings?

Hastings

Why was Richard I known as the Lionheart?

He had a transplant

How did food shortages affect the everyday lives of civilians during the First World War?

They made everyone hungrier

In pre-revolutionary France, who was the Dauphin?

Flipper

Which word beginning with C means a type of soldier who fights on horseback?

Centaur.

HISTORY

Name the English Queen who ruled from 1558-1603.

Princess Diana

Outline some of the virtues and flaws of the economic theory of the Invisible Hand.

You can't see what you're picking up.

What happened if the heir to the throne was still a child?

They had to make his crown a bit smaller.

What does a colliery produce?

Collies

Describe two of Galileo's inventions.

The telescope
Spying on his neighbours

Why did the Spanish finance the voyage of Christopher Columbus across the Atlantic?

They wanted to get rid of ~~tuna~~ him

What is a martyr?

You have them in salads

What is the name for a person who makes a pilgrimage to a holy place?

Jesus

Which American President instigated the 'New Deal' economic policies?

Walt Disney

Why did so many people go on pilgrimages in the twelfth century?

Because there was nothing else to do

Name 5 things that people in the Middle Ages believed to be causing the Black Death?

Black rats. Black food. Black water. Black dogs. Black paint.

Why did people wear masks during aerial raids in World War I?

So the security cameras didn't catch them nicking stuff

Discuss the relationship between the German crises in 1923 and the Beer Hall Putsch.

The crisis started because there wasn't enough beer.

What is meant by universal suffrage?

Astronauts getting injured in space
.

MUST TRY HARDER

In 1697, why were the Scots
annoyed by the Government in
London?

Because it was so rubbish

What factors affected Russia's
recovery after World War Two?

*Their recovery was slow because
they kept Stalin around.*

HISTORY

What were the main weaknesses of
the electoral system before 1832?

Electricity hadn't been invented

Outline the reasons why it is so
hard to defend an army against
guerrilla warfare.

Because they will
work for peanuts

What does the Anglo-Saxon word 'ford' mean?

A Car

What were the circumstances that led up to the Battle of the Bulge?

TOO MANY PIES

Why did so many bankers leave the profession after the Wall Street Crash?

Because they had lost interest

According to the Old Testament where did Adam and Eve live?

The Big Apple

MUST TRY HARDER

Briefly outline the causes of the
Great Depression.

My last set of exam results

What do you consider the main
reasons for Custer's defeat at the
Battle of Little Bighorn?

He was cowardy cowardy

What is meant by an anachronism?

Can you put the following kings of England in the correct chronological order – Henry II, William I, Richard II, Edward I.

In Ancient Rome what was a hypocaust?

An early hip replacement

Which invention did Alexander Graham Bell patent in 1876?

The bell

HISTORY

When did the 100 Years War end?

100 years after it began.

Why was William the Conqueror's son known as William Rufus?

It was his name

Who was known as the Hammer of the Scots?

Mchammer

What was the name of the Prime Minister during World War 1?

David Boy George

What were the main events leading up to the signing of Magna Carta?

Finding a pen

What is meant by circumnavigation?

It's something a Rabbi does to a baby

What was a Motte and Bailey castle?

It was the name of the company that built them.

The name of which Russian leader literally means Man of Steel?

Clark Kent

Which attack did Japan make on the USA on 7th December 1941?

9/||

Who ordered the murder of Thomas Becket?

The Mafia

Who were the British and French fighting in the Crimean War?

Criminals

Which battle saved Britain from imminent German invasion?

The 1966 World Cup final.

How long was the Berlin Wall?

It started in Berlin and went all the way across China to Puking

Why was the Korean conflict known as 'The Forgotten War'?

I don't remember

MUST TRY HARDER

What developed as a result of the Prague Spring in 1968?

The pogo stick

What is meant by the phrase 'lions led by donkeys'?

When the circus came to town

Why did Russia leave the First World War?

Russia left the war after
a massive attack of common sense

What was the plague that swept through England in 1665?

The ~~boobeenic~~ plague.

What was the 1918 peace agreement between the Allies and Germany called?

The Treaty of Vermicelli

What did Hitler call the book in which he outlined his ideas in 1925?

I'm Camp

What name did Hitler use for the single leader with complete power whom he said should control the German state?

Me

What was awarded to the best students in German schools?

a Swot Sticker

Women had more freedom in America following the First World War. What name was given to women who smoked in public and enjoyed new dances like 'The Charleston'?

Slappers

What were known as the 'July Days' in Russia in 1917?

The ones between the June Days and the August Days

HISTORY

What action in 1588 made Sir Francis Drake a hero?

He defeated the Spanish Ramraiders

Although he never lived in 10 Downing Street, who was Prime Minister in the eighteenth century when the building underwent 'The Great Repair'?

Pitt the Welder

MUST TRY HARDER

In Greek mythology, who was the brother of both Zeus and Poseidon and was God of the Underworld?

Herpes.

Who built the famous pyramids in Egypt?

THE PYRAMIDS WERE BUILT BY A BUILDER CALLED GEEZER

The inventor of the light bulb, also known as 'The Wizard of Menlo Park', was called Thomas Alva . . .

Dumbledore

The Indian city of Mumbai was renamed in 1995; what was it previously called?

Bumboy

What was first issued on 1st May 1840 and cost one penny?

The public toilet.

Who invented the Dambusters' famous 'bouncing bomb'?

Wallace Simpson

Which of the wonders of the ancient world is still standing?

Cliff Richard

According to legend, which creatures did Saint Patrick banish from Ireland?

The Leper cons

Which ancient battle gave its name to an athletics race?

The Battle of Marathon which is now known as Snickers

Which of Napoleon's victories had a chicken dish named after it?

The Battle of Vindaloo

What did Hoover commit US Government funding to begin building in 1931?

The vacuum cleaner

What was significant about Charles Darwin's sea voyage to explore the coastline of South America?

He travelled on a Beagle

What was the name of the German army's operation to invade and conquer Russia in 1941?

The Cold War

Who was England's first Norman King?

Norman I

Name Italy's powerful dictator from 1922-1943.

Musclelini

Who was executed at Yekaterinberg in July 1918?

The Tsar, the Tsarina and their children, the Tsardines.

What happened to many London school children during the Second World War?

They were evaporated to the country

What was the name of Hitler's secret state police?

The Gazpacho

What is the name of the famous British businessman who founded Virgin Airlines and Virgin Records?

Richard Virgin

By what electoral method are UK MPs currently elected to Parliament?

The first parcel post system

What is the main difference between Marxism and Neo-Marxism?

Neo

How do you think Benjamin Disraeli would do if he were leader of today's government?

Not very well. He'd be about 130.

What was one of the main criticisms of Albert Einstein in his long, illustrious career?

He should have used more hair gel

In the mid 19th century why did many early American settlers travel by covered wagon to California?

It was too far to walk.

During armed combat in the Coliseum who made the ultimate decision whether a gladiator would live or die?

The Roman Umpire

In which battle did Horatio Nelson die?

His last one

HISTORY

Who signed the American declaration of Independence?

Your fathers

Who was the father of the Black Prince?

Old King Cole

What is the main reason for Mazzini's failure to unify Italy in the 1840s?

His lack of success

An ancient poem describes how the Greek army concealed themselves in a horse. What is the name of the original source?

Troy Story

HISTORY

Why did Indian soldiers mutiny in 1857 when they were asked to bite the ends off cartridges and spit them out?

Because they tasted horrible

In the 18th century why did the Luddites set out to deliberately destroy farm machinery?

So they could claim it on their insurance.

Which military force did Herman Goering command during World War II?

The Luftwaffles

Which Ancient Greek physician is known as 'the father of medicine'?

Hiphoprates

What was Churchill referring
to when he said 'this was their
finest hour'?

The party at the end of the war.

Why did Nelson famously say
'I see no ships' at the Battle of
Copenhagen in 1801?

Because he'd forgotten his glasses.

What was most noteworthy about the Bronze Age?

It was the third best age.

What agricultural innovation was Charles 'Turnip' Towneshend best known for?

He invented the turnip

In 1845 what great disaster affected the entire population of Ireland?

The Eurovision Song Contest.

Where was US President John F Kennedy assassinated?

In the head

When was Rome built?

At night, because it wasn't built in a day

What marching song was adopted by the French republic in 1795 and still remains the country's national anthem?

La Mayonnaise

What factors contributed to the
Boston Tea Party of 1773?

The English government's heavy
taxes drove the settlers to their revolt

What impact did the building of
the railways have on the Industrial
Revolution?

People didn't need to drive their car to work.

MUST TRY HARDER

'Those who cannot remember the past are condemned to repeat it.' Give an example of the relevance of this quote to recent historic events.

Is that like, if I fail this history test I have to do the whole course all over again?